Pathways to Prayer

David Moffett-Moore

Topical Line Drives Series
Volume 20

Energion Publications
Gonzalez, Florida
2015

Cover Design: Henry Neufeld

ISBN10: 1-63199-185-X
ISBN13: 978-1-63199-185-1

Energion Publications
P. O. Box 841
Gonzalez, FL 32560

energion.com
pubs@energion.com
850-525-3916

To all who have prayed with me and for me:
family, friends and parishioners;
and fellow members of the
Academy for Spiritual Formation
and the Seeds of the Spirit program.
"Every day, every step, every breath, a prayer!"

TABLE OF CONTENTS

BEGINNING

This little volume is not a great theological treatise on the meaning and purpose of prayer, nor is it a scientific investigation on the function of prayer nor a psychological examination of prayer's impact or influence in our lives. It is a simple little devotional intended to offer encouragement for those wanting to grow in their prayer lives, with some suggestions on how to do so. It can be read for an hour or studied for a life-time, according to the reader's discretion. I pray that it may be helpful.

To be human is to seek for the holy, to look for meaning in one's life. To be faithful is to live "as if"; as if our lives indeed have meaning, purpose, value. These must be taken on faith, for there is no way to prove them. The Divine is so far above and beyond anything that we can comprehend, yet it is precisely what we seek. It is what the scriptures call "what no eye has seen, nor ear heard, nor human imagination conceived." It is what Rudolph Otto in *The Idea of the Holy* called the "mysterium tremendum," the mystery that attracts and compels us. This is what we seek in our prayer.

I encourage you to read the words slowly, reflectively, meditatively. Not because the words or thoughts are so great, but because that which we seek is great beyond knowing or naming. Let them speak to heart as well as head. Share your reflections with another, and share your own prayer experiences. I encourage you in your quest; may it transcend these notes and transform your life!

WHAT IS PRAYER?

Prayer is being wholly present to the sacred dimension that pervades and envelopes all of life. It is being fully and joyously attentive to the divine presence and divine process, so that the divine may be fully present to us, within us, and through us. Prayer is what connects us to the cosmos and to the great and gracious creative force that permeates and enlivens all creation. Prayer makes us part of the holy whole.

We are born praying. It is as natural to pray as it is to breathe, and as necessary. In prayer, we give as much as we know of ourselves to as much as we know of God. Understanding this, our first cry from the womb is an infant's heartfelt prayer, even though we do not know it, for in this cry we give ourselves fully to life itself. Our every thought, every feeling, every action, is a form of prayer. In a course of study on prayer, we do not so much learn to pray as remember how to pray, as we grow in our awareness of that great cosmic prayer that prays always from deep within us. To breathe is to pray; to live is to pray. To do is to pray; to be is to pray.

"Pray" is a verb, an action. It is something we do and something that is done within us. Prayer is relational, for prayer relates us to our Maker, to one another, to ourselves and to the cosmos. Prayer is what connects us.

We are conceived within the womb of another. Hidden within our mother, we grow and take shape. Through the umbilical cord we are connected not just physically but also emotionally, psychically, even spiritually. We taste what she tastes, eat what she eats, and feel what she feels. The mother and child connection is soul to soul. When we are born, we begin seeking that connection that has conceived us, longing for that intimate relationship that has embodied us. We seek community that is truly unity with another.

We are relational creatures, social creatures, and we belong in community. Prayer is what connects us with cosmos and Creator;

4

it is our umbilical cord to the divine. Prayer begins and ends with God, for we cannot begin to pray unless the divine spark is quickened within us. Prayer is embodied in and inclusive of all that we are. Anything that draws us closer to God is prayer, anything that heightens our awareness or deepens our experience of life. Prayer calls us more fully into the world, not out of it, for it is in and through creation that God first chooses to be known. God always hears, always is with us. In all of life, we are as much in God as once we were in our mother's womb.

Prayer is our heart's deepest yearning, our soul's sincere desire. Prayer is the longing that is within us. The Biblical word for spirit, "ruach" in the Hebrew of the Old Testament and "pneuma" in the Greek of the New Testament, is a full and all-encompassing word. It means spirit and air and breath. It is the wind that blows and in the lungs that breathe, in the nose that smells the odors and aromas in the air, it is the air itself. What can be breath and air and spirit? What but God!

The air around us pushes to get in, to enter our lungs; its force is gentle and subtle yet as precisely measurable as air pressure. Even so, the spirit pushes and pressures to enter us, enter our lives and enter our souls. Indeed, even as it is harder not to breathe than it is to breathe, so it is harder not to pray than it is to pray. As it is natural, effortless and subconscious to breathe, so it is to pray. As there is no wrong way to breathe, though our breathing may be improved, so there is no wrong way to pray, though we can grow in our praying.

We begin praying prayers of babes and infants, for that is what we are. We pray as children when we are children. We learn our bedtime prayers and table graces, offering simple verses that can be easily memorized, learned in our hearts. We know them by heart, which is a good lesson for us to remember as adults. We know by heart and are known by heart. We live our lives in the heart of God. Later we learn more formal prayers, longer prayers, and more eloquent prayers. These are certainly appropriate as we mature, but they are not better prayers, however much they may reflect our growing maturity. We may even learn to pray extemporaneously: with our own words, our own thoughts, our own feelings, we learn to express ourselves.

At some point we pray our first prayer that is truly heartfelt. This prayer may be a prayer of confession, when we are truly, earnestly sorry for something we have done or not done. It may be a prayer of petition, begging to the heavens for what we feel we cannot live without yet cannot attain on our own. We pray passionately and powerfully, pleading for our cause. We pray with tears, perhaps with quaking, putting all of who we are in that moment into that prayer, a prayer that truly consumes our whole being. It may be a prayer of thanksgiving, complete and humble adoration of the handiwork of God, gratitude for God's gracious and abundant blessing of our lives. Whether confession, petition or thanksgiving, it is a prayer that envelopes us, that offers our true and whole selves to the fullness of the divine presence, a prayer that is truly our prayer.

We pray the Our Father, the prayer that Jesus taught us. But do we really pray it or merely repeat it? Many scholars say it is an outline to prayer, an invitation to prayer, a map for prayer, that each petition may become a paragraph in actual use. The earliest Christians prayed the Lord's Prayer three times a day: morning, noon and night. Imagine how our lives would change if we incorporated not just the words but the spirit of this prayer into our lives as regularly as we take food to eat. Imagine tasting the food of eternity as frequently as we feed on temporary nourishment!

Does our prayer life mature as we mature? Do we allow our prayers to grow and develop or do we keep them stunted? While the prayers of our childhood are certainly good and acceptable prayers, they are the prayers of children. Adults need adult prayer, prayer that can express who they have become, not who they once were.

God is our holy lover, the one who seeks us and longs for us and yearns for us even as we seek and long and yearn for God. God loves us with an overwhelming love, a love that all the universe cannot contain. God comes to us, to be with us and to be one with us and to invite us into union with the divine.

God is like the wine merchant who has a very fine vintage and offers us free samples so that we may enter in and want more. God will tempt and test, entice and embrace, coax and coddle, call and beckon to us. Indeed, all of creation is God's great cosmic welcome mat, inviting us to join with God in the inner chamber. Why delay?

Prayer is conversation with God, not just to God. Prayer is not our wish list or shopping list, nor is it our lecture to the Almighty. It is good for us to talk to God, but not enough. We also need to take time to listen. Prayer is conversation and conversation is two way. We have two ears and one mouth for a reason! Listen twice, speak once.

Samuel heard the voice three times over, waking him in the night. Finally he said, "Speak, Lord, your servant is listening." Elijah went to the mountaintop to be with God. There was an earthquake, but God was not in the earthquake. There was a fire, but God was not in the fire. There was a whirlwind, but God was not in the whirlwind. Then there was the still, small voice, the sound of silence. Elijah covered his face and lowered his head, for in that silence was the voice of Eternity. The psalmist writes, "Be still and know that I am God," and again, "burnt offering and whole offerings you do not desire, sin offerings you do not require, but an ear you have dug for me. I am here to do your will."

Prayer is communion as well as conversation. Just as prayer is more a listening than a speaking, prayer is more a being than a doing. Prayer is being with God, spending time mindful of the divine presence that is always with us, around and through and within us. Prayer is allowing the boundary that separates us from one another and from the divine and even sometimes from ourselves, to fade for a while, to lose ourselves in the great oceanic bliss.

We think of payer as a doing, as something we do. Prayer is also something that is done within us. Prayer is being as well as doing. We are human beings, not human doings. Prayer is not just what we do, it is who we are, the very essence of our being. As Thomas

Merton wrote, we mature in prayer as an apple matures and ripens in the sun: not by doing, but by being, by staying attached to the tree of life. Prayer is a thing we do, but it is so much more. Prayer is who we are. We are created to be living, conscious prayers.

PRAYER IS NATURAL AND NORMAL

Prayer is our soul's sincere desire. It is our deepest need met by God's greatest, most gracious gift. It has been said that whatever is our greatest desire, our ultimate commitment, that for us is as God for us. Likewise, our greatest desire, our strongest yearning, our life's focus is for us our prayer.

Prayer is two way communication, talking with God and not just talking to God. More than giving God a laundry list of our wants and thoughts, prayer is communing heart to heart with the power of the cosmos, the cause of creation, the great Beingness beyond all beings, the "I am" of Moses (Exodus 3:14).

In today's parlance, prayers are "close encounters of the fourth kind." Not only talking about God or talking to God or talking with God, prayer is being with God, allowing ourselves to simply relax and enjoy the company of the Creator of the cosmos, the Almighty Eternal One, the Source of all being, the ever-speaking Word, the life-giving Spirit, the Force and Cause behind all that is, was and will be.

Our task as Christians is to bring God into the world, to make real, evident and tangible the divine presence that is always beneath, before, beyond all else. Ours is to work and live in such a way that the presence of God is made known. We are living reminders of God's presence in the world, faithful witnesses of our Lord Jesus Christ. We offer our witness of Christ in the world through our daily lives: our work and play, our family and community life, all that we do testifies of our faith in Christ. Our acts of compassion, our involvement in the social concerns of our community, are all pieces of evidence of our faith that we submit before the world.

As St. Theresa of Avilla said, "Christ has no hands now on earth but your hands, no feet but your feet, no eyes but your eyes. Yours are the eyes through which Christ looks with compassion

9

upon the world, yours are the feet with which Christ is to go about doing good. Yours are the hands with which Christ is to bless, now."

But how are we strengthened for our task? How are we to be fed and nurtured for our journey in this world? Through our prayer. Our prayer life feeds us. Our prayer enables us to live lives of faithful witness. Our prayer gives us the strength and the courage to do and the wisdom to know what and how to do. Prayer is the essential act of the Christian life, the one necessary fact for the Christian. We can pick and choose where we work, the jobs that employ us, the places we live, our hobbies and recreations, how we will be active in our community. But, above all else, before all else, supporting all else, we must pray.

The disciples witnessed the full life of Jesus. They saw him eat, drink, walk, sleep. They witnessed the miracles and healings, feeding the thousands, cleansing the lepers and raising the dead. They heard all his teachings, his commandments and parables. They did not ask to do any of this, they did not ask to feed the masses, heal the sick or raise the dead, not to tell stories, solve riddles or speak more boldly. In all their time with Jesus, they only asked him to teach them one thing: "Lord," they asked, "teach us to pray" (Luke 11:1)!

The good news is that prayer is the most natural act for both our spirits and our bodies. It is as natural to pray as it is to breathe. What is more, Jesus prayed as naturally as a child breathes.

From time immemorial prayer has been spoken of as the breath of the soul. The air envelops us. The air of itself seeks to enter us and, for this reason, exerts pressure upon us. It is more difficult to hold our breath and to not breathe than it is to breathe. We need only allow our lungs and muscles to do what is natural for them and what they were made for to breathe and bring life into our entire body.

The air our souls need also envelops us at all times and on all sides. It is in God that we live and move and have our being (Acts 17:28). Prayer is the breath of the soul, the spiritual organ by which we receive the life of Christ into our parched and withered hearts.

10

THE PRAYER LIFE OF JESUS

Prayer was not just a preparation for Jesus; it was an inseparable part of the whole fabric of his life. He preceded the crises of his life and followed his struggles with prayer. Prayer was so much a part of his life that the places in his ministry are identified by it: "Boats from Tiberias came near the place where they had eaten the bread after the Lord had given thanks" (John 6:23).

Sometimes Christ prayed in triumph, as on the Mount of Transfiguration when his whole appearance was transformed as he prayed (Luke 9:29). Sometimes he prayed in grief, as in the Garden of Gethsemane, when he prayed with such earnestness that he sweat blood (Luke 22:44). He spent whole nights in prayer (Luke 6:12), rose long before dawn to pray (Mark 1:35), withdrew at sunset to pray (Mark 6:46-47). He began his ministry by going into the wilderness for fasting, prayer and discernment. In the death throes of his agony on the cross, he prays with simple trust and full commitment, "Father, into your hands I commend my spirit" (Luke 23:46).

Again, the only thing that the scriptures record the disciples asking Jesus to teach them, is how to pray (Luke 11:1). If we let him, Jesus will teach us still.

Constant Prayer

In the scriptures we are urged to pray constantly. Paul writes, "Pray constantly, rejoice always, give thanks in all circumstances, for this is God's will for you in Jesus Christ" (1 Thessalonians 5:16-18). In a sense, each breath is prayer just as each day is pilgrimage. Our challenge is to grow in our awareness of this existing reality. The reality is that our lives are a prayer; our quest is to grow in our mindfulness of this reality.

Our first step is simply to slow down. We live in a very fast paced, outwardly focused society that can also be obsessed with the physical, tangible and very superficial, not looking at depth and meaning. The call to prayer is a call to meaning. To heed this call, we need to be attentive to the moment, to be where we are. Attentiveness is part of the call to prayer in every religion and in the writings of the mystics in every religion, culture and time.

This is what Simon and Garfunkel sang about in The 59th Street Bridge Song:

> Slow down, you move too fast;
> you've got to make the moment last.
> Just kicking down the cobble stones,
> looking for fun and feeling groovy.

Instead of fun, we are looking for fullness. Instead of feeling groovy, we seek nothing less and nothing other than feeling the presence of God in our midst. To accomplish this, we do need to slow down and make each moment last.

Be present to the presence of the Presence in the present! Be aware of the existence and nearness of the One Who Is, in each passing moment, the eternity revealed in the instant.

Prayer is feeding on God's presence. It is not only reading the words on the page in scripture or devotional writings, it is inwardly digesting them, ruminating on them, mulling them over and calling them to mind, so that the meaningless markings on the page become for us living words, words of life and fullness.

As a cow munches on the grass, swallows it, and then calls it up in her cud to chew it and digest it again, and then again and again through each of four stomachs until it is final absorbed into her being, so we ruminate on the Word, reading it slowly, letting it sink into our subconscious, then calling it to mind and reflecting on it again and again until it becomes part of who we are. Prayer is ruminating!

As infants we can first only take milk; our systems are not capable of digesting solid food. We take milk from bottle or breast, then from a cup. Next we move to pabulum, food more soft than solid that yields more sustenance than the liquid milk and that our bodies can digest. Finally we move to solid food and at last, meat. Milk to pabulum to solids to meat; as we grow, we gain. As we grow in our faith, do we feed ourselves the solid sustenance of a mature faith or do we stunt our growth and starve our nourishment by staying with the softer stuff of our less mature youth?

As we eat, are we aware of the nutritional value of our food? Do we consider the vitamins and minerals we receive, the protein and carbohydrates? Of course not. Yet the food still nourishes us. The spiritual nutrition we gain from our prayers is nonetheless real even if we are not consciously aware of it. Our prayers feed us even when we don't know it, just as our food still feeds us without our thinking about it. Do we spend as much time and energy feeding our spirit as we do our body, our soul as our belly?

Of course, as there is junk food and snack food, there may also be junk prayers or snack prayers, prayers that are offered in the moment but lack the strength to sustain us over long periods. We need to pray prayers that can provide for our long term spiritual health and well-being, prayers that feed the soul with the stuff of eternity, the stuff of the fullness of God in our time and place.

Lectio Divina and Centering Prayer are ways that can help to slow us down and open us up to the Presence in our present. *Lectio Divina* is a slow, reflective, devotional reading of a short passage of scripture in order to get the fullness of its meaning for our current situation, reading the Bible as God's personal message to us for that day. Read it over a few times and read it aloud, making sure we say and hold each word, let them linger. Read for some word to hook our attention, some word to speak to us from the printed page. Then we can enter into a silent period of Centering Prayer. Breathing in long, slow, deep, steady breaths, we let our body slow down and rest in the Presence. The purpose of this prayer is not to speak or share or even be aware, but simply to be. To be silent and to be, to listen and to be. Be with the One Who Is. We take a word with us to help us center again when we are distracted. The phrase "deep peace" may help, or simply the name "Jesus" or any name or word that calls us to God. *Lectio* and Centering are helpful in becoming constant in our prayers and becoming ourselves living prayers. More will be said about both of these pathways later.

Another helpful tool is memorization and repetition. Repeating words over and over is a way to free the mind, to pray with the mind in the heart as the Orthodox Christians say. We may have the Lord's Prayer memorized, favorite passages of scripture, and perhaps classic prayers of the church. Repeating them is a way to help form us in their image and feed us from their spirit. The repetition can be a path to help us become at one with the One.

Early Christians took the injunction for constant prayer quite seriously. They developed patterns to help the spiritual pilgrim be in constant prayer during the waking hours of the day. But how to pray when asleep? They believed that if one prayed while going to sleep and then continued that prayer upon waking, one could train the subconscious to be in prayer during sleep. Our subconscious is a part of us, and while it is below our awareness, it may yet be trained. If we can train our subconscious to be in prayer while we are sleeping our subconscious may then serve to call us to prayer throughout the day, that we may more fully become living prayers.

There is a story of a pilgrim who seeks out a monk known for his holiness. The pilgrim confesses to wanting and seeking God, but to little avail. The monk takes the pilgrim to a river and they enter it. The monk grabs the pilgrim by the head, pushing the pilgrim underwater and holding that head beneath the surface for some time. The pilgrim thrashed about and finally the monk raised up the pilgrim and asked, "What did you want, more than anything else?" "Air!" gasped the bewildered pilgrim. "When you seek God as you sought air," replied the monk, "then you will find God." How deep is our desire?

Other tools that can help us to become constant in prayer include the breath prayer. This is a short prayer that takes us one breath to pray, that we can repeat with each breath. It might be a passage of scripture or a line from a hymn or song. An ancient form of the breath prayer is the Jesus prayer: 'Lord Jesus Christ, Son of God, have mercy on me, a sinner." This has been used at least since the 4th century by the Desert Fathers and Mothers. It is a little long for one breath, but that may serve to help slow us down. Long, slow, deep breaths help us relax and become more mindful.

The arrow prayer is another such tool: this is a short prayer for a specific purpose, cause or person. We aim the arrow of our prayer in a petition and send it forth, shooting it towards our intention.

There is a connection between attention and intention. Attention may be more passive, like active listening with our whole being. Active listening is a form of listening that focuses on the listening, on hearing what the other person is saying, not just their words but their ideas, attitude, emotions; to fully hear the person of the other. As Martin Buber would say in *I and Thou*, hearing the other as a "thou" and not as an "it." Too often we think about what we are going to say when the other person is through rather than really listen to what they are saying. Active listening focuses our attention on the other, and paying attention is a good thing.

Intention considers our own desires and purposes in our approach. It means focusing our energy and effort on the object of our desiring. Both attention and intention heightens our awareness and focus our energy; attention is more outward and other oriented, intention looks within ourselves.

There is an awareness in our growth in prayer. Remembering the warning of the crossing guards on our way to school, we stop, look and listen. Before crossing the street or railroad tracks, we stop look and listen. In each situation we face and before each person we meet, we stop, look and listen. Each moment holds within it the potential of all eternity, if we but stop, look and listen. Each stranger we meet may be an incarnation of the Holy One, if we will stop, look and listen. Every spot on earth may radiate with the glory of the heavens, if we but stop, look and listen.

God is nearer to us than we are to ourselves, knows us better than we know ourselves, and loves us greater than we can love ourselves. God's steadfast love toward us knows no bounds, God's constant faithfulness no limits, God's abiding presence no barriers. God is constant. In our prayers, we seek that same constancy.

Praying Through the Day

"Great is thy faithfulness, great is thy faithfulness; morning and evening, springtime and harvest, new mercies I see; great is thy faithfulness, O Lord, unto me." We sing the hymn. We pray constantly and we pray through the day. We have a pattern of morning and evening prayer and of night time prayer and vigils.

We begin and end the day in prayer. We can pray through the activities of our daily living. We can have prayers upon rising, prayers for dressing, prayers for cleaning, grooming and bathing. Prayers for eating. Prayers upon leaving the house and returning again. Prayers for our commute and prayers for the work place. People are notorious for doing many things while driving: eating donuts, drinking coffee, shaving, putting on make-up, talking on the phone or working on the computer. Imagine what it would be like if everyone during rush hour spent the commuting time communing with God? We are spiritual pilgrims on a life of pilgrimage, and that drive is part of our daily pilgrimage. Pray for the person in front and the one in back, and the one who just cut in. Pray for our co-workers and those with whom we have appointments. Pray for our companions and our competitors. And at the end of the day, pray that it may all be in the loving embrace of Almighty God, and sleep with a clear conscience.

The scriptures speak of prayers at rising, at noon, at evening, at night and during vigil. The Jews had prayers three times a day and pray the Shema upon rising and resting and upon leaving and returning: "Hear O Israel, the Lord, the Lord our God is one, and you shall love the Lord your God with all your heart and soul and strength" (Deuteronomy 6:4-5). Our Islamic brothers and sisters have five set prayer times daily. The medieval church had eight hours for prayer: matins at midnight, laud at sunrise, prime at six, terce at nine, sext at noon, nones at three, vespers at sunset and compline at bedtime. The Didache, "The Teaching of the Apostles," from the earliest decades of the church, recommends praying the Lord's Prayer three times daily: morning, noon and night. Remember the call from our childhood to stop, look and listen. How do we mark our time for prayer? How do we maintain our vigilance and alertness? In the garden, Jesus urged his followers to stay alert and keep vigilant; how do we heed that call in our daily lives?

In his classic *Practicing the Presence of God*, Brother Lawrence of the Resurrection calls us to practice God's presence in all the mundane ordinariness of our lives. Practice the Presence while weeding the garden, while peeling potatoes, while scrubbing pots and pans, while running errands. He lived to sense God's presence in marketplace and courtyard as much as in the choir stall of the chapel. "I would not so much as stoop to pick a stalk of straw from the ground but for the grace of God."

There is the story of a rabbi who had a student ask why so few people can see God and sense God's presence in their lives. "Because they do not look low enough," was his answer. God is a God of the ordinary and the everyday.

We certainly pray when we gather for worship. Corporate prayer means praying as the body, and the church is the body of Christ whether gathered or scattered. The Upper Room in Nashville, Tennessee, has a small prayer chapel beside its larger "Upper Room" chapel. Over the doorway is a sign, "Alone with God." An Orthodox Christian chuckled on seeing it. "Alone with God? We are never alone! All the saints are always with us." In the Apostles' Creed we say we believe in the resurrection of the dead, the communion of the saints, and the life everlasting. In the Eucharist we join our voice with all those on earth and in heaven. Do we mean what we say? Do we realize what we are saying? All those in all times and all places: past, present and future; those who have gone before us and those who are yet to come. This is corporate prayer, praying as the body and giving voice to the cosmos.

There is more to prayer than the words. Prayer is relationship, a "being with" more than a "talking to." That is why attention and intention are so important. Effective prayer does not depend on technique or formula or recipe. Sometimes the most effective prayer is simply one word: thanks, wow or help.

Prayer needs to include some self-examination. In Jesus' parable it was not the Pharisee who was praised but the publican who confessed, "Lord, have mercy on me a sinner." In his methodical approach to everything, John Wesley, the founder of Methodism, advised reflection for self-examination that rotated through the days of the week, asking different questions each day and providing a thorough and on-going course of "examen," spiritual reflection and evaluation.

Two simple memory aides for prayer may be in the ACTS of prayer, Adoration, Confession, Thanksgiving and Supplication, where petition is prayer for ourselves and intercession is prayer for others, and PRAY: petition, requests, adoration and yielding. These are described in detail later.

By whatever means and following whatever pattern, if we are to grow in our prayer we need to have some method of exercising ourselves daily in prayer and using the events of our lives as calls or reminders to prayer. If we want to be in good shape physically, we need some discipline to exercise our bodies. If we want to be in good shape spiritually, we need some discipline in our devotional life. Praying through our lives begins with praying through the day.

PRAYER AND PERSONALITY

The Shakers had a greeting dance that they used in opening their worship, "The Christ in me greets the Christ in thee and draws us together in love." That is a nice way to begin worship or acts of service and good words to remember each time we meet another. If we greeted each person as if they were Christ, we might be more likely to actually see the Christ that truly is in each person we meet.

In this way we can train ourselves to be living prayers, so that prayer is not just what we do but who we are. Growing in prayer is not just learning to do prayer, it is also learning to be prayer. Prayer is as much about being as it is doing!

We are each unique creations of the Divine Lover. If God makes each snowflake unique, that often melt before they touch the earth, how much more must we be unique, who are destined for eternity. If God creates over 7,000 different species of mosquitoes, how much must God delight in diversity! If God even makes our fingerprints unique, how much more must God make our person-alities unique, which are so much more a part of our inner being. Being different in personality, it is also reasonable that we may be different in our prayer. We have different ways of praying, different approaches to prayer, different patterns in prayer. We are unique and so are our prayers.

The Myers-Briggs Type Indicator (MBTI) and the Enneagram are two ways for looking at our uniqueness. Myers-Briggs offers sixteen different personality types, each of which has its own ap-proach and perspective and each has its own preferences in prayer styles. The Enneagram offers nine different personality types. There are many resources for either approach, according to our own preferences and what we find most helpful and meaningful. My approach is to use what is helpful and discard what isn't helpful.

The Myers-Briggs Type Indicator draws on the personality preferences of Jungian psychology; people have four preferences:

20

introvert or extrovert, sensing or intuitive, thinking or feeling and judging or perceiving. There is no good or bad, right or wrong, none are better than others; they are simply preferences. In our society, roughly 75 % are extroverts, 60% sensing and the other two preferences are about 50/50.

Roughly 50% of church goers will be Sensing-Judging; they are the guardians and stabilizing traditionalists. These are the ants in Aesop's "The Ant and the Grasshopper." An approach to prayer that they may be more comfortable with is from the Ignatian tradition. Place yourself within the Biblical scene. Where do you find yourself in the passage? What is your internal perspective? In reading the passage of Martha and Mary, Luke 10:38-42, how do you identify with Martha? How with Mary? In the parables and events of Jesus' life, place yourself within their framework.

Maybe a third of parishioners will be Sensing-Perceiving. They like to celebrate and experiment. These are the grasshoppers in "The Ant and the Grasshopper." They will enjoy a walk in the woods, admiring great works of art, listening to fine music. St. Francis preaching to the birds will be an attractive image for them. They would prefer to recast favorite scripture stories into the present setting: what would they look like in our time and place?

Ten percent or less of parishioners will be Intuitive-Thinking. These are the rationalists, they want to understand the mysteries of faith and be able to make sense of it all. Theirs will be a more intellectual prayer pattern, one that requires them to think things through. They might be the religious reporters, asking "who, what, why, where when." As an example, in Mark 8:34, what does Jesus mean in stating the doctrine of the cross? What crosses do we carry, how do we carry them? How can we and do we deny ourselves?

Fifteen percent or so of parishioners might be Intuitive-Feeling. They seek authenticity and meaningfulness and have the greatest drive for self-development and spiritual growth. They will want a direct encounter with the divine. For instance, take John 3:16 and make it personal: "For God so loved (you) that God gave (you) God's only son that (you) might believe and that (you) might have eternal life." Or Colossians 1:26-7, "The secret of life, the mystery of the ages, is simply this: Christ in you (your name), yes, Christ in you (your name), bringing with him all the hope and all the glory that is to come."

If nothing else, I want to be clear that there are a variety of ways to pray, and each one of them is appropriate. Use what works. It is good to note that while roughly half of all parishioners are Sensing-Judging, 40% of clergy are Intuitive-Feeling. Churches tend to be extrovert and want pastors who are extroverts. Pastors tend to be introverts.

MANY PATHS, ONE CENTER

I spent some time as Spiritual Formation Program Director for a Catholic retreat center, an incredible honor for a Protestant pastor. I thought it important that I be able to experience Catholic spirituality from the inside, so I bought a rosary and practiced using it daily. It was a tremendous experience for which I am very grateful. I quickly learned that it was not my job to get anyone to walk my path; rather, it was my job to help them walk their own paths, in the confidence that if they grew closer to God in their way and I grew closer in my way, we would also grow closer to one another. The retreat center's logo was "Many paths, one Center." Many paths, many pathways, many patterns, many processes, yet it is all prayer.

There are active and passive prayers, prayers for resting and prayers for working. Prayers might be kataphatic, with words, symbols and images, or apophatic, without any words, symbols or images. Kataphatic prayer is prayer that uses symbols and is described as "positive." Apophatic prayer uses no symbols and is described as emptying or negative, the way of "unknowing." Our first prayers are as introductions or preludes, as we start by wading or tiptoeing into our spiritual experience. We grow in comfort and ease and confidence with familiarity and our prayers move from friendliness to friendship, conversing as friend with friend. In the depth of prayer we grow to be buoyed up by the relationship, by now grown deep and supporting and embracing us. In the intimacy of prayer, we experience union with the holy. Mystics of all religions share that divine union is possible, though it may be fleeting. Like all relationships, there are ebbs and flows in this living, dynamic relationship of prayer.

There is a story of a salt doll who encounters the ocean. It is strange and foreign; the doll cannot identify with it. "Touch and see," said the ocean. The doll touched the ocean and gained knowledge from the experience, though a bit of the doll dissolved into the ocean. Wanting more, the doll touches again, and again. Going deeper and deeper, the doll experiences more and more. Finally dissolving in the depths, the doll and the ocean simply say "I am!" Such is the experience of holy union.

Studies in biorhythm suggest that we should regulate our prayer time with our energy levels. Biorhythm and biofeedback is the study of our physical, emotional and intellectual cycles. If we want to give our best to God and be our best before God, we should see when our peak times are. If we are morning persons, our time of prayer should be in the mornings. If, like Garfield the Cat, we are allergic to mornings, it might be best if we not force ourselves to begin the day in prayer. Having a set time and a specific place for prayer helps us train our bodies and our subconscious to be ready for prayer at that time and that place. Listening to our bodies and knowing our energy levels helps us plan to be most attentive when we are most energized, a good combination for effective, fulfilling prayer.

Keeping a journal with our prayers can also be helpful. We have few enough maps of the road ahead spiritually; keeping a journal helps us see where we've been. Entries might be of the prayer experience or prayers themselves or of events of the day that affect our prayer. We might ask ourselves at the end of each day where and how we have seen God that day and enter our answers in our journal. Making regular entries and reviewing them from time to time helps in our self-awareness and can be part of our self-examination and self-discovery.

Having a spiritual companion, guide or director, or soul friend, is also helpful for our spiritual growth, a spiritual trainer like a physical trainer. We are not alone in the journey, and sharing it with another can be beneficial, someone we can bare our souls and share our hearts with, someone with whom we can be absolutely honest. The other may support us in times of doubt or drought and hold us accountable for our spiritual journey. St. Brigit warns, "A soul without a friend is like a body without a head."

Like other great mystics, St. Theresa of Avilla writes about three stages of personal spiritual growth: illuminative, purgative and unitive. The first sheds light upon our path, offering discovery and growth. The second burns to purify, offering examination and letting go. The third is our becoming one with the One, the goal of our desiring. Having climbed the mountain of our transfiguration and arrived at the peak of transformation, we then return renewed. St. Theresa's words live within us:

> Christ has no body now on earth but your body;
> No hands but your hands,
> no feet but your feet, no eyes but your eyes.
> Yours are the eyes through which looks out
> Christ's own compassion upon the world,
> Yours are the feet with which
> Christ goes about, doing good.
> Yours are the hands through which
> Christ is to bless, now."
> May it be so! Amen.

CLASSICAL PRAYER PATTERNS

The act of prayer is as old as humanity itself. The Indo-European word from which our word "God" derives is "gawatha," meaning to cry out or to invoke. So the word "God" is originally more a verb than a noun, more an act than a name.

One classical expression of Christian spirituality comes from the Rule of St. Benedict, established 1500 years ago and based upon even older traditions within the early Christian communities. It is called "lectio divina" or "holy reading" and based firmly on the reading of Scriptures. This includes four steps: lection, meditation (including both recitation and rumination), oration and contemplation. Translated, these would be: reading, thinking (both mentally and subconsciously), prayer and stillness. We first read the scriptures, then reflect upon what we have read, respond to it, and finally rest upon and within the scriptures. St. John of the Cross said, "Seek in reading and you will find in meditation; knock in prayer and it will be opened to you in contemplation."

In praying the scriptures, we need to first simply find a quiet place where we can be alone. Take time to relax and make the time you have committed to be truly consecrated. Read a brief passage of scripture, a psalm, parable or paragraph, enough to engage you, not more than you can digest. Read as if for the first time. Reflect on that passage. What in it shimmers before you and attracts your attention? What in it snags at you and catches you? Find a word or phrase that both works on you and you can work with. Spend time ruminating on the word or phrase; listen to it. Afterward, rest for a while and simply relax and let yourself be in God's gracious presence. Close with a brief prayer of thanks to God for the time and attention that God has given you. During the day, recall that word or phrase as a gift from God and let it continue to season and flavor your day.

For most of us, we know prayer as petition: giving over to God's care the joys and concerns of our lives, our wants and wishes, our thoughts and words. We also know the experience of lection, or divine reading, whether scripture or devotional material. Reading it in such a way as to nourish our hearts and not our heads, reading to experience the presence of the divine. We have all practiced recitation, recalling phrases of scripture, hymns, poems, or other devotional writing that has been particularly meaningful for us. Early monastic orders required candidates to memorize the entire psalter so that they could participate in its recitation during their community prayers. Likewise, we have all ruminated on these words, gone over them in our minds and hearts, working them over in our thoughts and allowing them to work us over and work themselves into our lives, even as yeast is worked into dough.

Meditation and contemplation are forms of prayer we are less familiar with. They are not intellectual forms based upon logical sequence. They are more heart-felt, working more on a subconscious level. The focus of meditation is simply to spend time with God, to set apart a period of time to relax, breathe deep, and allow ourselves to rest in the presence of our loving, powerful Creator. Psalm 131 may be a description of this:

> O Lord, my heart is not lifted up,
> my eyes are not raised too high;
> I do not occupy myself with things
> too great and marvelous for me.
> I have calmed and quieted my soul,
> like a weaned child with its mother;
> My soul is like a weaned child within me.
> O Israel, hope in the Lord from this time on
> and forevermore!

Contemplation is being at one with God, which is the goal of our atonement in Christ. It is the experience of losing our selves in the Self of God, being so aware of God's presence that we lose sight of our own. "Atonement" means "at-one-with."

It is important to remember that the monastic orders also believed firmly that their work was a living out of their prayer and not separate from the act of prayer: "ora et labora," "pray and work." Likewise, our own work is a living out of our prayers in and through our daily lives, our witness of the sincerity of our worship, our behavior bearing out what we really believe.

Gregory the Great, a pope of the 6th century, summarized the Christian contemplative tradition as "resting in God." We may think of prayer as thoughts or feelings expressed in words, but this is only one expression. Contemplative prayer is the opening of mind and heart, our whole being, to God, the Ultimate Mystery, beyond all thoughts, words and emotions. We open our awareness to God whom we know by faith is within us, closer than our breathing, closer than our thinking, closer than our choosing or feeling, closer than consciousness itself. Contemplative prayer is a process of interior purification leading to the experience of divine union.

Centering prayer is a method designed to facilitate the development of contemplative prayer by preparing our faculties to cooperate with this gift.

The root of prayer is interior quiet. Contemplative prayer is a prayer of quietness, an experience of God's presence as the ground in which our being is rooted, the source from whom our life emerges at every moment. Centering Prayer facilitates a movement from more active modes of prayer: verbal, discursive or affective prayer into a receptive prayer of resting in God. Centering Prayer is meant to enrich and complement other forms of prayer, not to exclude or replace them. Centering Prayer is at the same time a relationship with God and a discipline to foster that relationship. It is Trinitarian in its source, Christ-centered in its focus and ecclesial in its effects; that is, it builds communities of faith and bonds the members together in love.

Here are some guidelines for Centering Prayer:

1. Choose a word as the symbol of your intention to consent to God's presence and action within you, such as "Jesus," "Deep

28

Peace," "Come, Holy Spirit," "Loving Presence," "Come, Lord Jesus," etc.

2. Sit comfortably, eyes closed, relax and focus on your word as the symbol of your consent to God's inner presence.
3. Breathe long, slow, deep, steady breaths.
4. As you become aware of thoughts, feelings, memories, images, etc., simply return gently to your focus word.
5. At the end of your prayer time, allow a few minutes to gather and re-direct yourself.
6. Allow 15-20 minutes, twice daily if possible. (First thing in the morning and again in late afternoon or early evening. Some prefer immediately upon rising and just before sleeping).

The principle effects will be in our daily life, how we live when we are not consciously praying, and not in the actual periods of prayer themselves.

SIMPLE WAYS TO PRAY

Maybe all these theories and techniques seem to be just too much information! Too complicated, too much to think about and worry about and try to get the right things in the right way and the right order when all we want to do is just pray! Certainly there is no one right way to pray. There are as many different ways to God and ways to pray as there are people on this planet. Here are some simple ways to pray.

THE ACTS OF PRAYER

The ACTS of prayer is an acrostic prayer pattern based on the call of the prophet Isaiah by God in Isaiah 6 and the interaction between the spirit of the prophet and the Holy Spirit of the Living God. The acrostic of ACTS stands for Adoration, Confession, Thanksgiving and Supplication.

When we first come into God's presence, we are filled with a sense of worship in adoration, praising God for the attributes of God made known to us in God's grace and power.

We then move naturally to our own condition before God, and in humility are filled with a sense of confession, being honest about our failings and shortcomings before the wonderful perfection of God. We admit that we are not God.

With the foundation of an honest relationship with God, we can't help but give thanks for all the gifts, blessings and benefits we have received from God's amazing grace and abundant love.

Having given thanks for what God has already given us, it is then appropriate that we offer to God's care and attention what our heart next desires. Through supplication, we offer to God prayer petitions for ourselves and others. Supplication consists both of intercession, our prayers for others, and petition, our prayers for ourselves. We prayerfully lift up the needs of the world before the

Creator of the world and we share in God's own concern for all creation.

Too many times we skim over the adoration, confession and thanksgiving and merely offer God our wish list. God is not a cosmic Santa Claus waiting for us to sit on God's lap and tell God all we want God to do and give. God is described by Jesus as "Abba," the loving, gentle, powerful parental figure that watches and dotes over the helpless infant and whom that infant trusts implicitly and adores completely. It is more accurately translated "dada" or "papa" rather than the much too formal "father." God knows us better than we know ourselves and knows our needs before we ask. More than anything else God wants us to be God's heavenly children. This prayer pattern can help us spend more quality time with our loving God and also help us move beyond thinking of and experiencing prayer only as mere petitions.

PRAY

PRAY is another acronym that can serve as a memory aid to guide our prayers. In this form, we begin with our petitions, a natural beginning. We share with God our wants, needs, concerns. Moving from ourselves, we offer our requests: intercessions on behalf of others, lifting up God's world and the needs of the world before the maker of the world. Adoration is always a good thing to include in prayer: understanding and experiencing the greatness that is God, thanking God for being God and for all the blessings of God that we have received. We end the prayer time in simple, quiet, restful yielding, giving God time and space to work in our lives, even subconsciously.

STOP, LOOK AND LISTEN

Another simple prayer pattern is one we learned in kindergarten: stop, look and listen.

First we stop. Take time apart and time away. Find a quiet place where we can be quiet, within ourselves as well as in the world around us. Breathe long, slow deep regular breaths. Let ourselves rest, relax and just be.

Look at the world around and our place in it. Not mere physically looking, but examining ourselves, our words and deeds, our thoughts and feelings, our actions and attitudes. What have we done, said and experienced? Where has God been with us, when and how? Where and how have we been absent to God's abiding presence?

Finally, listen in the here and now, in the present moment when we are focused on the Divine Presence and the Divine Moment. What is God saying to us in the present moment? Where is God calling us? What is God's still, small voice saying to us and asking of us?

Stop, look and listen. Three simple steps that can take us into the heart of God. Maybe all we need to know about prayer, we learned in kindergarten!

BREATH PRAYERS AND SCRIPTURE

I have used a variety of scripture verses as part of my Breath Prayer practice. They can be used as affirmations and as a way for us to focus on a positive thought rather than a negative worry. Again, Breath Prayers are prayers that may be slightly longer than a single breath; most scripture verses fit well within this parameter. Here are some samples.

For Healing: "Touch me Lord, that I may be healed."

"Create in me a clean heart, O Lord." (prior to heart surgery)

When showering: "Remember your Baptism and be thankful." "The power of the Holy Spirit work within you, that being born of water and the Spirit, you may be a faithful witness of Jesus Christ."

When washing: "Wash me from my iniquity and cleanse me from my sin. Purge me and I will be clean; wash me and I will be pure."

Brushing teeth or gargling: "May the words of my mouth and the meditations of my heart be acceptable in thy sight, O Lord, my rock and my redeemer." I've a dental hygienist as a daughter in law who reminds me to spend at least two minutes brushing my teeth. I can mentally pray the Lord's Prayer with my lower and then my upper teeth and pray through those two minutes.

When dressing, "put on Christ." Underwear: the girdle of God's strength; socks: the Good News that God reigns; pants: my shame is covered by God's glory; shirt: the breastplate of righteousness; belt: the belt of truth; shoes: the Gospel of Peace. Watch: I live by God's time; pocket cross: the sword of the Spirit which is the Word of the Lord; change: I serve God, not Mammon; billfold: my identity is hid with Christ; keys: the keys of the Kingdom; handkerchief: I breathe the breath of God; jacket: I am clothed in Christ; tie: I am yoked with Christ; glasses: I see with the eyes of Christ, I see Christ in others; hat: the helmet of salvation; briefcase: the shield of faith; comb: be the image of Christ for others, live so others may see Christ in me; pen/pencil: Christ, mark my life and through me, mark others; calendar: my time, my life is God's; cell phone: speak, Lord; your servant is listening.

In walking, taking stairs, driving, waiting: "Jesus" with each step, each breath; "Lead me, Lord, lead me in your righteousness, for it is thou, Lord, thou Lord only, that cause me to dwell in safety." "Thy word is a light unto my feet, a lamp upon my path."

At mealtime or while fasting: "We live not by bread alone, but by every word that proceeds from the mouth of God." "My meat is to do the will of God." "Blessed are those who hunger and thirst for righteousness, for they shall be satisfied." "The Kingdom of God is not meat or drink, but righteousness, peace and joy in the Holy Spirit." "Taste and see that the Lord is good!" "I am the bread of life, whoever follows me will never hunger, whoever believes in me will never thirst." "Keep me hungry, Lord, for the filling that only you can give."

Throughout the day: "Rejoice always, pray constantly, give thanks in all circumstances, for this is God's will for you in Jesus Christ." "The fruit of the Spirit are these: love, joy, peace, patience, kindness, goodness, gentleness, faithfulness, self-control; against these there is no law." "Whatever is true, honorable, just, pure, pleasing, commendable; if there is any excellence, anything worthy of praise, think on these things."

Growing in Prayer

While any prayer is good prayer and it is natural and normal for us to pray, as much as is our breathing and a vital part of what makes us human, it is also true that we can grow in prayer, in our understanding and experience of prayer.

We begin as babies, mimicking what we see and repeating what we hear. We bow our heads and fold our hands because we see others do so. As we learn to speak the language that others speak around us, we learn to repeat the words we hear them say. As they repeat the same prayers daily, we learn to repeat those prayers, without necessarily knowing what the words mean. It is important for our children to see us pray, so that they can learn from our modeling.

Next we learn to recite the prayers we have memorized. "Now I lay me down to sleep." "God bless Mommy or Daddy." "Bless this food to our nourishment." This is a beginning of developing one's own prayer life. We learn to adapt our prayers to fit our own situation: blessing our pet dog or cat or goldfish or changing our prayers with the seasons.

As we become increasingly comfortable praying, we begin praying outline prayers. We have a prayer pattern we are familiar with; there are points we want to include in our prayers. We may move from our family to our community to more global concerns. We might start with joys and move to concerns.

Eventually we engage in free-form prayers, prayers that are more conversational in their style. We are talking to God, sharing our days and our lives with our Divine Maker and Holy Lover.

The transition from talking to God to talking with God may seem obvious enough, but it represents a tremendous change in our understanding and experience of prayer. When we are talking with God rather than merely talking to God, God becomes much more an active participant in the prayer process. We learn the importance of listening in our prayer time and not just talking.

Listening to God in our conversational prayer moves us into prayer as being with God, an intimacy of presence that requires no words. It is learning the truth of the saying, "I pray not to change the world, but that I may be changed." Learning to be with God opens us up to experiencing prayer as communion with God, as being "at-one-with" and "as-one-with" and opening us up to that great cosmic unity of being at one with the One, the mystic experience of the divine-human encounter.

Anthony Bloom, Metropolitan in the Orthodox Church, trained as a physician, member of the Underground during World War II, experienced as a diplomat, after years of public service and personal devotion, wrote *Beginning to Pray*. We are all just beginning to pray!

Continuing

Our prayers never end. We may say the "Amen," but there is no end! "Amen" means "so be it" or "make it so" or even "I second that motion!" The word itself connotes a continuing rather than an ending.

Our prayer never ends. If we pray constantly, pray through the day and through our activity during the day and pray with each breath and each step, our life as a prayer is always continuing and never truly ending.

I hope you have found this little book helpful. I hope it may help on your way and on your path. As I said in *Life as Pilgrimage*, "life is a journey from the place of our birthing to the place of our rising." May this have helped you make a few steps on your pilgrimage.

I urge you to continue your journey, your search for self and for Spirit. There follows a listing of books for further reading. Find something that speaks to you and keep listening; find something that calls to you and keep following. There is an awesome, wonderful, overwhelming Love awaiting. Enjoy the journey!

TOPICAL LINE DRIVES

Straight to the Point in under 44 Pages

All Topical Line Drives volumes are priced at $4.99 print and 99¢ in all ebook formats.

Available

The Authorship of Hebrews: The Case for Paul — David Alan Black
What Protestants Need to Know about Roman Catholics — Robert LaRochelle
What Roman Catholics Need to Know about Protestants — Robert LaRochelle
Forgiveness: Finding Freedom from Your Past — Harvey Brown, Jr.
Process Theology: Embracing Adventure with God — Bruce Epperly
Holistic Spirituality: Life Transforming Wisdom from the Letter of James
— Bruce Epperly
To Date or Not to Date: What the Bible Says about Pre-Marital Relationships
— D. Kevin Brown
The Eucharist: Encounters with Jesus at the Table — Robert D. Cornwall
The Authority of Scripture in a Postmodern Age: Some Help from Karl Barth
— Robert D. Cornwall
Pathways to Prayer — David Moffett-Moore
Render to Caesar — Chris Surber
The Caregiver's Beattitudes — Robert Martin
What is Wrong with Social Justice — Elgin Hushbeck, Jr.
Why Christians Should Care about Their Jewish Roots — Nancy Petrey
From Words of Woe to Unbelievable News — Robert D. Cornwall
Constructing Your Testimony — Doris Horton Murdoch
I'm Right and You're Wrong: Why We Disagree about the Bible and
    What to Do about It — Steve Kindle
Stewardship: God's Way of Recreating the World — Steve Kindle

Forthcoming

God the Creator: The Variety of Christian Views on Origins — Henry Neufeld
Ruth and Esther: Women of Agency and Adventure — Bruce Epperly
From Here to Eternity — Bruce Epperly

Planned

A Cup of Cold Water — Chris Surber
Christian Existentialism — David Moffett-Moore

(The titles of planned volumes may change before release.)

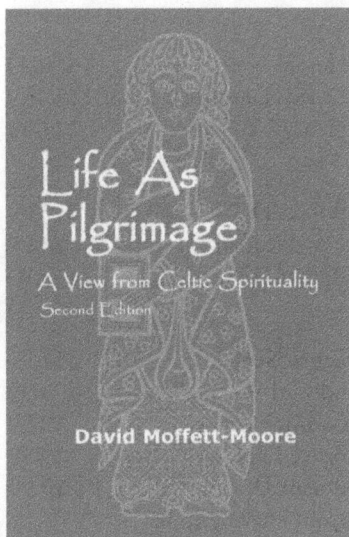

With the Peregrine Falcon as a symbol and the Celtic tradition for inspiration, [Moffett-Moore] provides us wonderful guidance for our pilgrimages.

Dr. Douglas E. Busby
Author of *Coming Together for Spiritual Healing*

I recommend Dave's Study Guide for students who are not afraid to encounter scripture, examine personal faith and enlist in practical service for Christ.

Rev. Ronald Devenport
Pastor
Mill Creek Baptist Church

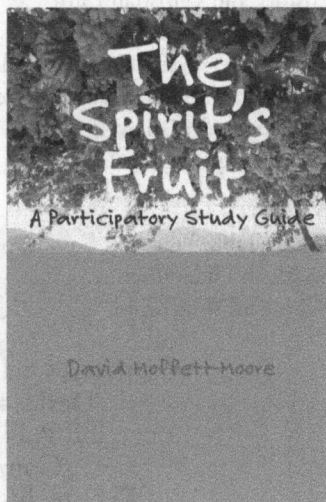

MORE FROM ENERGION PUBLICATIONS

Personal Study
Finding My Way in Christianity	Herold Weiss	$16.99
The Jesus Paradigm	David Alan Black	$17.99
When People Speak for God	Henry Neufeld	$17.99

Christian Living
Faith in the Public Square	Robert D. Cornwall	$16.99
Grief: Finding the Candle of Light	Jody Neufeld	$8.99
Crossing the Street	Robert LaRochelle	$16.99

Bible Study
Learning and Living Scripture	Lentz/Neufeld	$12.99
From Inspiration to Understanding	Edward W. H. Vick	$24.99
Luke: A Participatory Study Guide	Geoffrey Lentz	$8.99
Philippians: A Participatory Study Guide	Bruce Epperly	$9.99
Ephesians: A Participatory Study Guide	Robert D. Cornwall	$9.99
Evidence for the Bible	Elgin Hushbeck, Jr.	

Theology
Creation in Scripture	Herold Weiss	$12.99
Creation: the Christian Doctrine	Edward W. H. Vick	$12.99
Creation in Contemporary Experience	David Moffett-Moore	$9.99
Ultimate Allegiance	Robert D. Cornwall	$9.99
History and Christian Faith	Edward W. H. Vick	$9.99
The Church Under the Cross	William Powell Tuck	$11.99
The Journey to the Undiscovered Country	William Powell Tuck	$9.99
Eschatology: A Participatory Study Guide	Edward W. H. Vick	$9.99
Philosophy for Believers	Edward W. H. Vick	$14.99
Christianity and Secularism	Elgin Hushbeck, Jr.	$16.99

Ministry
Clergy Table Talk	Kent Ira Groff	$9.99
So Much Older Then ...	Robert LaRochelle	$9.99
Wind and Whirlwind	David Moffett-Moore	$9.99

Generous Quantity Discounts Available
Dealer Inquiries Welcome
Energion Publications — P.O. Box 841
Gonzalez, FL 32560
Website: http://energionpubs.com
Phone: (850) 525-3916

www.ingramcontent.com/pod-product-compliance
Lightning Source LLC
Chambersburg PA
CBHW011749020426
42331CB00014B/3328